,

mollusc

HELEN CLARE

First published in Great Britain in 2004 by Comma Poetry
Comma Press, 3 Vale Bower, Mytholmroyd, West Yorkshire HX7 5EP
www.commapress.co.uk
Distributed by Inpress
www.inpressbooks.co.uk

A CIP catalogue record of this book is available from the British Library

ISBN 0-9548280-0-3
Comma Press gratefully acknowledges assistance from the Arts Council of England
North West, and the Regional Arts Lottery Programme.

Set in Bembo by XL Publishing Services, Tiverton
Printed and Bound in England by SRP Ltd, Exeter

For Patrick
who let me be

ACKNOWLEDGEMENTS

Some of these poems have previously appeared in *Rialto*, *The North*, *The Reader*, *Ambit*, *Smoke*, *Magma*, *MsLexia*, *Brando's Hat* and *Manhattan Review*, as well as the anthology *First Pressings* (Faber). An earlier version of 'Lotl' won First Prize in the Yorkshire Open Poetry Competition 1998. 'Tired' won First Prize in the Poetry section of the London Writers Competition, 2002. 'Making New Materials' was a winner in the Lancaster Litfest Competition, 1999. 'Reception' was a Runner Up in the Daily Telegraph Arvon International Poetry Competition 2000.

CONTENTS

Comet Keeps its Date with Death
The Guardian, Monday 18th July 1994

I heard the world might end on my wedding day,
began my own countdown
in yards of silk and lace,
and champagne roses (seven).

Five hundred billion miles away
a comet fractured into twelve,
spiralled towards a planet
drawn closer – still closer.

Telescopes waited, spacecraft
hung beyond the atmosphere.
I iced a cake, stitched a hem,
slept in curlers.

At three o'clock we met as strangers,
stood separate, side by side, then touched.
The twelve became twenty.
Eighty voices sang Jerusalem.

In the garden I became the hub of the universe;
people circled, brushed against me,
dusted me with kisses, wishes.
I clutched a silver plastic horseshoe.

The sun in its July nearness
shone for me; unblocked by clouds
it stirred the air, warmed my skin,
the pavement. The roses wilted.

Later, taking refuge from the throng,
the stultifying heat of a blinded room,
I sat on a roadside bench, waited
for a fireball on the dark side of Jupiter.

Saw nothing,
took it as auspicious.

Trouble

It starts with the breeze
of a rumour that twists round town,
needling our backs, like someone stepped
over our graves. Closure. The steel
stripped from beneath our feet. Hangings,
gassings, drownings peak at three
a month, before the line drops to the trough
where the rest of us survive.

It starts with a change
in the tide. Ore is scooped from the Baltic.
Cheaper. Quicker. The gravid ships
beach, coastal towns thrive. Here
we're too far inland, we scratch
deeper into the wound of the land, yield less
of the crumbling orange earth that feeds the furnace.

It starts with the overflow
of men from the granite North. Uprooted
wives and children are carried in the rush
for work, sink into lush soil. Houses mushroom
in rings round the village, brick gives way
to concrete, grass to tarmac.

It starts with the boot print
of factories on the fields, the plume
of yellow light from the furnaces. Orange dust
smuts the sheets. Throats are tempered
with ale, steel is quenched nail hard.

It starts with one man
his horse, leased land. Base metal
changed to gold across his palm. Bricks
pressed from the earth beside the precious stone.

It starts with the ground
on which we walk. The minerals of the crust.
Iron of our blood. Carbon of our flesh.

The Singing Lesson

I tuck my bag neatly beneath the polished table.
My feet have puckered the thick polythene sheet,
but left the Chinese rug beneath untouched.

She makes me *ning* my scales, feeling the bridge of my nose
for vibrations. When I am more advanced
I will be permitted to *ning-nu*. To do so now
would risk displacing the voice from its seat in the sinus.

She hammers with one sharp nailed finger.
She does not like my diction, unstrings
the guts from my *g*s. My *ings* no longer ring.
Later the tape recorder rattles on mahogany
My small voice resonates. She is pleased.

She teaches me to breathe, raising the ribs of my back –
a heaving bosom, as she says, would be too disconcerting.
I concentrate, hold my breath, let out a steady stream
that would bend but not snuff a candle flame –
and fart. She is not disconcerted.

I tip into her hand a fistful of silver –
she charges on a sliding scale. In the hall
her stroke-skewed husband gives me sweets,
the old half sighted dog shuffles his rolling belly into my hands.

She watches me as I descend the terraced garden.
Birds are singing. I hum. I can feel the air in my lungs.
The vibrations in the bridge of my nose.

The Witch's Hat

I'm in the playground, where the Witch's Hat
once stood, toeing the burst tarmac boil
where the central pole was torn away.

I walk the Spirograph path it creaked,
and crouch to gauge the level of the brim –
polished by shorts and woollen tights.

It seems that I jumped off as you rode on,
flying breathless over the curving earth
as the Witch's Hat slips from its mount

corkscrewing down as you cling on,
your bubbled breath set in tarmac –
as a dimpled fairy ring that seems to be

a place where small feet scuffed the ground.
It drew you down, so far, so deep
that wherever I walk, you are beneath my feet.

Turning Over

I sit on her left. The audience on her right.
The piano's angled – for them she's half back
half side. The singers see her face.
I watch the notes, the ones she plays
and the ones she reads – two bars ahead,

hear only her part – harmony, and melody too,
if you care to pick it out from the chords.
The singing's froth like the lace
we sewed on my skirt to fake a flash
of petticoat. *Snowing in Paris*, the men would say

in London, when she was young. Before me.
Before the singers she knew turned up on the radio.
There's no snow here. My black hem's straight,
my black sleeves are tight. There's nothing to hang
as I turn the page in those free-flying

moments before she catches her note.
It's the left arm you use, even though she's
on your right. Feels wrong at first, but that's how
you reach over and not across, your arm poised
like a long high C. That's all there is to it,

apart from reading two bars ahead, and knowing
which tunes will set tears behind her glasses,
that no-one else sees. Tunes from back then.
I've a hanky up my sleeve. It's my first haircut.
I'm allowed blusher – her Flower Drum girl.

Sometimes her glasses fall down her nose
her perfect narrow nose. I've tried sleeping
with a clothes peg on mine. I like it best
when she says I take after my grandma
though I never thought she was pretty.

Intervals – I carry her bag so she doesn't lose it.
Weak tea and dry scones catch
in my throat. The men tell jokes about nuns
and rabbits. As if we didn't learn that stuff.
Everyone knows about tenors anyway.

At the end there'll be applause, people
want to touch her so I know to stand back.
Still, she'll not let me out of her sight
and I get to carry the flowers, slitting the cellophane
so the orange pollen feathers my black top.

There's calls of goodnight, smudges of damp
on the worn steps, ivy round the door
or maybe honeysuckle. My mother's breath
on the back of my neck. Lily of the Valley.
Yardley. It takes a while to adjust to the dark.

My father chivvies the pedal, the engine
strains at the air. The flowers go in the boot.
I hum and the car sings its response
to my cheek through the blue metal door,
holding its diminished chord almost too long.

Spotting

It is late summer. He is my father. Tonight I have danced
in the old church hall, to a tune about Narcissus. Step
developpé – the gradual unfolding of the leg, the slow point
and place into the future. We are parked on a mud street,
on Back O'Moss. The still night smells of fern.

He is visiting a lady doctor. He needs to talk about his mother.
There were nothing but fields and farms here when he was the boy
who knew the names of tractors and watched the harvest.
I danced in a long cotton dress with a print of strawberries
I stitched myself. I want to be Isadora Duncan.

My mother played the piano for me, knowing when to stretch
the tune and when to quicken, without looking. The examiner says
I have a good body for this work. My little sister has good legs.
One day I'll drive down this street, new and tarmacked
to watch the woman who mothered my father wait to die.

First arabesque, arms outstretched – holding your own beating heart
like picked fruit. We have left my mother with my sister.
I sit in her seat. In a distant city, years ahead, I'll stop my car,
after watching other people's children dance, and open the sun roof
because the air is the nearest thing to dancing en pointe.

My hips will set splayed. Well into old age I'll demonstrate proudly
that I can still make fifth position, have bookcases from the floor
to the ceiling, as I've glimpsed from the car. My father returns
ready to talk, holding my face in his gaze. I wrap the ribbons
round the shoes in my lap. It is almost autumn. I am his daughter.

Play Suspended

Bat and helmet have been cast near the wicket;
pad, sock and boot sloughed like snake skin.

A batsman curls by his crease, waits,
as a figure scurries from the dressing room.

The field collapses like a fingered web. Men
straggle and bunch, two in the foreground sit.

One has crouched for hours, in the thicket
of wild shots, quick as a twitching hare,

the other perched in a line of catchers,
watchful as birds on a pasture fence.

Now, knees bent, resting on back-stretched arms
they mirror each other, as if pivoted,

as if each might reach for the others weight
with the rocking gait of a nursery game.

Glimpse

And sure, the England cricket team have them:
scraps of grey
above the boot's side scoop
behind the pad's fat lip;
thin cotton
stretched across a bundle of bones,
packed tight as kidney stones;
worn to cobwebs at the heel; wrinkles
forming as the elastic strays
from the thick ribbed fold;
blurring the knife-pleat tendon
as the body weighs forward. It's said
that early in the season
wives open drawers, see them clean and rolled,
laid out like days,
and think of ankles,
sunless as the sunken stems of bluebells.

Biology

Day after day, her heels click on the wooden floor,
the thick cotton of the labcoat rustles
as she reaches for jars behind glass. She knows
them all, the snake skeleton, bleached
slender and white, the rat pinned open like a tent,
the frog displayed and labelled, the skull
with the hole in the forehead, though she jokes
that brains come out best through the nose.

She keeps her scalpel greased and sharp, can slice
clean through the white of an eye of a cow,
pick out the lens with forceps, hold it like a prize
between finger and thumb of her thin rubber glove,
knows the best way to catch worms with soapsuds
and the best way to kill them, watches them coil,
tight-lipped. In the freezer, there are fish
the lungs of sheep, the hearts of cows.

Each night she leaves the coat with its nameless smears
on a peg, throws the gloves into a bin.
At home she changes her shoes for boots,
walks the dog, smiles at the way his hind legs quiver,
throws him sticks and stones, feeds him treats
of chocolate and yellow strips, lets him lick her face,
scoops him into her arms, thinking nothing of the mud
thinking of nothing at all, but his heat, the smell of skin.

Lotl

is what we call her. Once she had a mate called
Axy, but he chewed off her legs, which is how
she comes to be lurking in the tank at the back
of Biol 2. Watching my girls. Or would be
if she weren't nocturnal, and pretty near blind.

And dim. Though she's beautiful in her way.
Long as your forearm, greeny black and squishy
as a jelly baby. Staying like a young Salamander
all of her life while this lot snicker and whisper
as we run through secondary sexual characteristics

again. In the spring, she'll be fat with eggs,
though not a male let near her. They'll be out of here
by then. Pushchairs, rent books and maybe even
a bloke to fit in the Moss Bros. The nearest Lotl
ever got to any of that was two days fun and games

her little legs floating at the top of the water.
They'll grow back. And come September
there'll be another lot in here looking
through the same windows. Tapping on the glass.
Lotl might live for thirty years.

But I'll be here to look after her, even over the summers,
turning into the kind of teacher that says
'I taught your mother'. Let the tank go dry
and Lotl's gills wither away, and her skin browns,
her nose gets fat, and she breathes

for the very first time. Iodine would do it too.
The girls say, *Go on, be a laugh*. I'd stir the stuff
into the tank and wait, watch her change,
see her crawl from the water, taking all her weight
on her soft new feet. But I say, *No*.
No. Once it's done there's no going back.

Making New Materials

Take solution *A*. Decant
into beaker. Flirt
with its chloroform fumes.
Watch it swirl, sluggish
in dragon breath curls,
colourless clear
on colourless clear.
Add *B*, aqueous, hear
its lighter fall. Watch
it skate across the surface,
settle. Take a glass rod.
With the vertical stab
of a tailor's stitch,
plunge through fluid
to the partition
of *A* and *B*. Lift
straight and true
the way you lift
a paint-oiled brush.
No drag. Slowly.
Something has congealed
like custard skin
on the rod; a line
leads to the source
between liquids. Balance
the rod on beaker. Twirl
between thumb and finger
like a magicians wand.
Steady. *A* and *B* constantly meet
react, are drawn to the rod.
The thread winds even, smooth.

This is nylon.

Mycelia

Parasols of fungus rising in the night,
floating on air like jellyfish
are mostly water. The rest a skein
of membrane held bloated and firm.

Slowly, after the dust of spore is wafted away,
more gently than the heat of a hand,
the water becomes steam and seeps
into air. The floating cups sink,

fungus shrinks back to its threads
weaving through moist earth,
becoming soil, the black clumping
on them, velvet on chenille yarn.

Amid the violence of earthworms
they stitch through the soil, embroider
the tunnels of ant hills, unpicking
cells of leaves to skeleton lace.

They scrawl their soft patterns
on the carcasses of beetles, trim
away the torn flanks of mice
until everything passed is peeled down

to its tiniest parts, to its tumbleweed
molecules of protein and fat
and caught in the fabric of fungus,
as it trawls its net through the earth.

Shell-Like

Your flat's an amnion you fill with sound
to drown the whine you always hear. Head
in hands, your shoulder sinks beneath my touch
as if you'd concertina fold, until
I'd tuck you in my pocket like a letter.

So let's leave. We'll fall back to a time
before your voice slipped down its scree slopes
to baritone, that evening after orchestra
when you slid from dado to skirting, the glass door
melting into pleats at the noise you never made.

Forget the honeycomb chords you pulled
from our mother's baby grand, the sustain pedal
you pressed so hard its steel wire tendons
sagged and made the piano tuner suck his teeth;
wipe away those times in the Hillman Imp

blanked by the back of our parents' heads
sounds ripening in our mouths, each plucking
the note that came next in the tunes we built,
and finding them a minor third apart.
The wordless language we spoke unravels

until there's only the note the tiny mollusc
of your inner ear sings to itself as it listens.
A note as specific as a finger print
or the oil-slick screen at the back of the eye.
I sometimes seem to hear it in the silence.

Snakes and Ladders

The call to DNA,
to King's. It pulls Rosalind from Paris.
It's 1950. She's young,
walks lightly.
It feels like spring.

The skill, to hold each molecule
as if patterned from popper-beads,
in her secret skull space,
to zoom, rotate
predict the spattering left on an X-ray plate
by the ricochet of electrons
on internal surfaces.

Daily isolation.
She's the only female,
the only Jew.
Denied the soft seats
of the gentlemen's dining room,
she must take her food
and wander.

This second form she finds,
that coils and leaps from the plate,
that must be glued in place
before examination. It's the kind of luck
she combs for. She names it *B*.

Wilkins. Squirms, hisses
softly at this stockinged intruder,
arches away from DNA.
Begins the quiet transfer
of information to an opposition
she cannot imagine.

Caution. She steps carefully,
stacks up her evidence
before she leaps.
Ignores the call
of the charismatic *B*,
though she sees its double helix.
Finishes the first form first.

Watson, Crick, handed the plate
that completes the picture,
are struck by inevitability,
take to their tools, piece together
a molecule from sheet metal shapes –
a ladder snaking upward
from their desk.

In watery contemplation
atoms clump to molecules,
attach to each other,
float into position in a framework
and then, when the final fragments
fail to fit, are wafted away.
She's nearly there.

Watson and Crick.
DNA, the double helix.
She admires its easy beauty,
does not recognise her labour
in its backbone curl.

She hitch-hikes round the dead sea.
Then moves to Birkbeck college.
Still bomb-torn, there are buckets
under drips. Her colleagues are Bolshies.
They make her laugh.
She beams her pin prick of light
into the dark world of the virus.

Deep inside, the quiet transfer
of information from cell
to daughter cell
falters. Her DNA
is fallible. As it uncurls
splitting along it's rungs,
a slip that trips a switch
and suddenly cells divide,
bloom like algae.

She shares her bed
with a wriggle of kittens,
dines in red silk,
rests her bones
in the Crick's spare bed.

Pain coils across her abdomen,
exposes the shape
and position of her organs,
clear as on an X-ray plate.

At the last, she takes on
the Polio virus,
flaunting the immunity that cancer brings.
She does not lose faith
with a world of test and proof
that lets her slip away.

It is not like coming home,
not even like landing
on the final square.
More like the pieces being swept
into the box and the lid shut,
and the dull sense
of having been cheated.

I have Become a Stranger to my House

It's all my fault. All those trips back and forth,
leaving it, like a dog in quarantine.

It's forgotten my smell, can't quite slip back
into the pattern of my days. At night

its noises wake me – rattles and whines
I can't quite place. Reaching through the net

of sleep, I find the switch a hand's breadth
from where it used to be. The room has swirled,

everything settled again like sand, though light
pokes in through what should be a solid wall.

By day, I can never find a pen, my books
are packed away, my hairbrush in another town.

I open drawers, find gadgets I never bought.
A stranger's photos tumble from the stack

behind the cupboard door. The furnishings
have suddenly faded, the paint has thinned.

I see the walls the way they were before
I came. The house dreams of different paper,

of other colours. Each Friday as I leave,
it watches me silent, half-curtained.

All weekend it waits eager for the sound
of someone else's voice.

The Irwell

Not far from here the Irwell rises, little more
than rain water trapped between thin soil
and a sandstone hill.
                              Then, further down,
rivulets run, slight and shallow, their surface
crumpled by blades of grass and sedge.

Impossible for anyone to know
the point at which marsh becomes river.

Once, I was held here, not stagnant,
but leached with the stuff of this place,
smelling of its earth.
                              And now, I am going;
it's taken months, ticking off lists, held forever
on a phone line, snatching letters from the mat.

Impossible for me to know
the point at which my leaving began.

Only that days from now, I
and my belongings will travel the road
that tracks the Irwell,
                              West and South,
past Manchester, and beyond the reach
of any river I know.

Borderlands

Some roads loll
across the thinning towns

where houses perch on rock
like wafers in sundaes

and sheep snuffle
for grass roots in thin soil.

People watch their feet,
they take small steps

on cushions of air –
in their nightmares they tumble

off the edges and lie beyond
twitching like late bees.

When no-one is looking
they practice standing on one leg:

a drunk forgets and sings
and the wind steals his voice.

Dark falls and all is rolled
into the mouth of the hillside.

Canteen

That were summer it started. Ferranti's canteen.
I seen food for what it were. Frozen fat
on carcasses, giant tins o peaches
all slimy an crumbling. Right the way
ter shinin pink bacteria like froth
on inside of that tank of a dishwasher.

After a few week I knew that even Rum Baba's –
all gold an sticky an temptin at first
were nowt but slops from moment
they first hit yer tongue. An littul pool
of syrup round base like sweat
round yer bum on bus ride home.

First job each day were sarnies. Six of us
in a line. Margein, Fillin. Liddin.
Cuttin. Boxin. Sealin. Six pair o legs
stuck out, like one o them Chinatown dragons.
An all knocks an gurgles an beat of its heart
yer could never stifle not even wi shaggin.

I were quick. Not just wi sealin –
my bit o sandwich run that shined
print off mi finger on otplate
but clearin too. Twenny bi two
trays stacked wi plates, and bigguns
on top o littluns an me just a blur

in mi pumps an blue nylon slip,
hummin, movin, bein in wavelength
that were never switched on. An good at wipin –
not in circles like you'd think, but end
ter end, then end ter end the other way,
obliteratin where you'd been. And Brenda

big woman on Hospitality wi me
took a likin ter me, slipped milk
left over on a Friday into mi bag.
Yer'll fade ter nowt, she'd say, wheelin
that china clunkin trolley in ter boardroom,
hips swingin like a muffled bell.

Company

He's been with me a while, now –
my great-great-grandfather, the clog maker.
He means to comfort me. Tells me
how he dragged his family, his Lancashire trade,
to Wales. The mountains tumbling
through tiny windows, not like
the Pennines shrugging a shoulder
in invitation. How his wife wept.

He talks about leather and lasts, holds
up his hands, sinewy, pale,
the thumbs a little squared. They remember,
he says, every shoe, like the wooden
base of the clog keeps every step taken.
A man holds himself and his family
in his hands. His trade is his home.
In Wales, those days, even his name.

Only sometimes, I could do without it.
Those bad jokes, about finding my feet,
the way he pffs at my cheap shoes,
the air whistling around the nails
in his mouth. And wages like they are,
these days, he sighs. And forever
making edged remarks
about great-great-great-grandchildren.

Which is why it was such a relief
when a friend's great-grandfather –
the cheese-maker turned up at supper
the other night. Perfectly at home
in her London terrace. Watching us read
the fat content of the brandy butter
with that gallic curl to the lip.
You could tell he thought us daft.

Amiable enough though. Quite touching
in fact, that soft browned hand,
just a stroke from her shoulder.
And not bothering with the white hat
or gloves or sliding metal probes
into the soft core, just breathing it in
with great noisy gulps. Passing it
to the children to eat from the round.

Neither man said much,
one having a mouth full of nails
and the other testing the Camembert rind
with his teeth, and there being
no language shared between them –
only a look, a smile of recognition
and as we left, a low laugh
that wisped round the room like pipe smoke.

Against Insomnia

So once you've added to the list
of things you thought you'd lost,
but never had, leafed through the folio
of beds you've slept in, and chosen
the place you'd like to be tonight,
then thank the God of Sprawl
for single occupation of a double bed.
Summon up the silence of the only man
who held you without touching you.
Confess. Let guilt stain your breath.

Tired

As if in the school sick room with the sound of the secretary's heels
on polished wood fading away, the dials on the old teak wireless
turn and it tunes in once more to a voice with the pitch and fall
of your mother's.

        The needle scrolls through London, Welsh and Midland
you get off the tube at Holborn or somewhere, after trying not to feel
the breath of someone chewing gum by your ear, and you've hummed
a slow tune so hard, you're walking it against the street's quick pace,
no idea the ground you've covered.

        Somewhere down my street, once
a boy was arrested – his cuffed hands held out like a prayer and the muscles
of his back stretched as if they might burst into wing and it seemed
the policeman said *Hey* a little softer than usual.

        And now this girl
knocks on the door saying, *I need to talk to a woman*. It's raining hard,
she's no coat or umbrella, and no-one's around, although through the wall
they're singing hymns – you can hear the organ, but not the words.

On Every Tube

there is a woman crying noiselessly and a woman
carrying flowers. Other women avert their gaze
from the woman crying. Their eyes are drawn
to the flowers – sometimes glancing up at the face
of the woman carrying the flowers. They know
that tomorrow the woman carrying the flowers
will be averting her gaze from a woman crying
noiselessly, that only yesterday the woman
crying found her eyes drawn to the flowers
another woman was carrying, that one day
they will not be looking, or not looking,
but will be women carrying flowers or crying
noiselessly. On every tube there is a woman
who does not believe this, who suspects
that there is one who is always crying, noiselessly
and one who carries flowers every day,
and that she will forever be looking or not looking
or trying not to look, fixing on her hands.

Reception

The voices she hears come from unseen mouths.
She imagines the hungry beaks of fledglings,
the gullet stretched and pale. She disgorges
the few words she has, repeated so often
their consonants adhere to the vowels
of neighbouring words. Nobody hears.
They're waiting for another voice.

She likes taking his calls, hopes for the edge
of a word as she connects, or better still
the red light that says his line is busy.
Later when the light blinks off, she'll call
read the message to him. She'll picture his face,
close her eyes to catch the colour of his voice.
He'll thank her. Say her name.

Sometimes with a man, a man she has met
and shared a meal with, or maybe a film,
she tilts her face to his, from habit or forgetfulness.
She imagines tightness at his mouth's corner,
the way saliva beads, feels his breath
on her face, his need heavy on her mouth.
She is wordless, her tongue drawn from her.

His mouth is different. She can't tell why. Maybe
it's the story he told her about the cricket ball,
the metal taste of his own blood, the sharp
edge of enamel, the gum cavity collapsing
under his tongue. Maybe it's that ruminant
twist to the jaw as he speaks, the way
his lower lip rests on his finger as he listens.

If she's lucky he'll come for a package or a fax
just as the phones have hushed. He'll lean
on the high desk and watch as the lazy words
form themselves in her mouth. Occasionally
the words tumble from her teeth and tongue
so fast its hard to wait, to choreograph
all these thoughts, this little time, into a conversation.

Sometimes he'll come and the lines will be so busy
she can't even lift her face. Other days
there's no faxes, no packages,
or he'll pick them up when she's at lunch.
Or he'll be so busy, he'll never emerge
from the office she's never seen
behind the glass doors.

Those days, she thinks of his mouth moving
as he talks, imagines catching his words in her mouth,
coming so close, she'll touch his tongue
at an 'L' sound. One lunch time, she buys a dress
the exact blue-grey of his voice.
She wears it the next day, her hair bright on its shoulder.
If he notices, he doesn't mention it.

Bliss

Those were the moments you nearly touched something
close to the secret of the universe, but necessary.
Sixteen, your skirt hoiked over your arms, leaning
to the wall, a stray hair streaking up the damp tiles.

The world's little wisdoms in the combed grout,
the overlapping of three different linos on the floor,
the hollow where the door's worn through jammed
with paper, and love and hate penned and scratched

on yellowed gloss. You're seven pints down, a few to go,
your bladder gives release, and the bones of your arse
know it all. The crack on your seat. The lap and hard-on
game. Eeeny meeny miny mo. Play the one

with the boob tube and the slack elastic? But still
you end up in the back of a taxi, with some loser,
the one guy of the lot with pigeon toes or something
and your head rattling against the thick cushion

and he holds you to him, and he's warm and anyway
right now there's nothing you wouldn't do
for a good night's sleep. So back at his place
that's the line you take, though nobody ever bought

jam for tomorrow. Your luck's really out –
there are squares of the Express hanging up in the john,
and come the morning you find the shower head's
not detachable. You go home chafing. But at least

the lager and black's as sweet on the way up
as on the way down, and you sleep on the bus.
Somewhere down by the Texaco garage
you remember that last night it almost ran clear,

and if you could only be quick enough
with the bit of your brain that makes like a fist
you'd catch it. The sun's come out. Later
you'll shop for nail varnish. Tonight's your night.

Dog Days

By now you're waiting for the heat to break –
it's built up in layers that the thin night rain
can't crack. You crave that other England –
the wet grass on your arse, the mad breeze
on the moor, the morning mist that burns off
if you're lucky. But more that that, something
needs to end – the tubes, the cars, the turning
of the days, the washing up, the labour
of your ribs, the sticky arms you've lain in.
You feel your own slow dying and the rot
of living flesh in the softening of your skin,
the rub between your thighs. But death
like you imagine it – dark, cool, floating
you'd settle for a sleep like that.

Belay

He's back. I've left him in the bath and come downstairs.
Everything's still packed. Rucksacks bulge
with pitons, spikes; the metal nuts that wedge in rock.

Only the rope spills from its canvas bag, thick
and muscular. It kinks as if it can't quite shake
the memory of the knots that held him.

Grains of other places rasp between damp threads
of lime and black. Upstairs those grains are loosed
from skin and hair, eased from the crevices of his nails.

I hear him call me; thread the rope through my fingers,
feel again his weight in my hands, see the rope uncoil
beside my feet as he reaches heights I'd never dare.

I let it go. Soon it will dry, release its grit to the carpet.
Later, one of us will vacuum, clean the bath. Now
I'll climb the stairs.

Watching the News

Smoke bursts from the base of jumbo Mechano
as a missile is fired across the desert. Feminist
literary theory is splayed where I dropped it. I guess
that he's behind the lens, knowing I could be as fooled
as the girl in his story, who leaning on a balcony
for a half-pissed party fuck feels her lover uncunt,
re-enter, sees him moments later waving from below.
I've the sound turned off, the Brandeburgs playing
as they were the time he filmed me, suddenly
singing along in a brief respite. I'll wait for his
commentary, his antipodean voice
growing stranger, the more it grows familiar.
There's Hagen Daaz softening, pieces of a snakeskin
corset waiting to be sewed. In another time his balls
slap against my arse. Our two worlds shudder.

Straw Dogs

Shit. The message he relays is brief. A bomb.
A place. An estimate of casualties. And still
I don't quite get it. A world I've never fathomed
has leaked into my living room. He understands.

Sex is snatched and purely genital. My grunting
rocks on grief. He crashes to my bathroom and back.
I hug him, let him go, hug him, let him go again.
The machinery's in motion now. I'm gripping air.

Love might be a brief slip of the tongue. He's gone
before he's left. I can't have half the night we'd planned.
Instead it's crime tv. Cheap chocolate and gin.
Muted. Waiting till the casualties are named.

Anchor Point

At least we're past all that – those days
when a late return from the rock
could draw a cry
that had me on all fours.

These days there's no call
for the splash of cold water,
the measuring of steps from the slam
of Landrover doors to his voice

in the stairwell, finding me
calm as the chamomile pads
I kept for my eyes.
Something has cooled

between us. It's easier, now
the lie has set like steel,
fixed so firm you could hang
a marriage from it.

Only, sometimes I'm woken
by the whirr
of rope slipping through metal,
faster than a hand's reflex.

Poem to be Left where a Father-in-Law Might Find It

Because you don't do aspirates
you've never called me by my name.
It's as if I'm wearing someone else's frock
nicely pressed, and probably floral.

I pen your name on every cheque:
its single syllable tucked
neatly into its final plosive –
the way you belt your trousers.

Which is Something Like a Love Poem

You phone to say you're nearly here
and it is like
the clock that's been stuck
with its finger twitching
neither progressing or falling
just got new batteries
which is like the toilet
that's been hiccuping all day
miraculously flushing
as if all the water in the world
is suddenly undammed and unfrozen
which is like spring
and petals uncurling
and later the heat tempting
pine cones to open
and spill their seed
which is like the powder
that explodes from puffballs
pinged by autumn rain
which is like squeezing a spot
that's been waiting for days
which is like farting in the bath
or stopping by a bush
on a very long car ride
feeling the fast steam of pee
and watching it darken the soil
which is like the flush of colour
when hot water is poured
onto jelly crystals
and all that was dry
is made plump and shiny
and then the jelly slips
from the mould with a slurp
which is like taking off
a too tight bra and dancing
which if you are very nice to me…

Flesh

At first all I see
is that belt to pubis
she's concave
as a china platter.

Under folded arms
I caliper pinch
the flesh on my ribs,

compare
her adipose layer –
a quarter of mine,
an eighth,

barely there –
a lipid clingfilm.

She talks, smiles
My teeth are exposed.

I'd like to disrupt,
the line of her
weigh her down
at the hip,
see her strain
at the seams.

She offers me
her open palms.
My arms unfold.

When she leaves
she hugs me.

I fit my chin
into the spoon
of her shoulder.

Geology

This is why the lead miners of Northumberland
call their veins *she*, and consider themselves artisans –
having split the earth's surface, they follow its faults
and seams to reveal the secrets of its history.

This is what I can give you tonight, parting my legs
to your eyes for the first time. I have not told you
that I dream of opening you up like a lily
and slipping a finger into your fragile core.

Honey I'm Home

Remembering how my mother sang
as she set the table, I lay out
vibes, ice-cubes, handcuffs, lube.

By the time I hear the key in the lock
I'm spread-eagled on the sofa,
blindfold, my mother banished.

Dirty

It's only after the sticky night
the oils, the toys, the photographs
I find the soap on the side of his bath –
Wright's Coal Tar: amber, medicinal, clear –
and recognise the smell that drew me here.

Bridal

If I leave the photos on the mantelpiece
and wrap my gown in polythene,

recline on pink faux fur or satin sheets,
would you unlace me with your teeth?

A Brazilian at Blake's

In the basement of Blake's old house
I'm laid out on paper, knickerless
a mirror facing my open legs.
Warm wax, skin held tight, the rip,
a fuzz of hair on linen, as fingers
staunch the tide of pain,
methodical, until a rubbered knuckle
slips beneath an outer lip.
Then I look, to see this touching
so precise and circumspect. Done.
I must admire her art – to find
it's innocence that's stripped away –
before I oil and dress, leave, to text
the sweet voyeur who I suspect
would happily have watched.
I prickle in the heat
trying not to think of Ruskin.

Slag!

The word lay on my skin. Cold. Viscous.
It would not wash off. Slowly it seeped
through my pores. Spread.

It lies on my tongue. Thick as fur.
The word. It rises like dough.
Blocks my mouth. Mutes me.

Your tongue must never touch mine.
I can feel it now. The word. Multiplied.
In your sweat on my skin.

Meat

Until one time you discover you have skin –
as he's pressing apart the steaks of your labia,
rolling all those tired words over you.

You dress in clean silk, leave him asleep
mumbling his curses, steal a smoke –
its film forming in the lining of your lungs.

Bondage

After all the kinks we've rolled through
we reach the last – yours to zip
and leave and mine to slit
my chest and hold the flaps apart for you.

One of These Days

It will be bright and cool. I'll wear cotton.
Fresh, as if the miles were moments away.

You'll be in the garden, with muddied knees,
your face soiled where you paused to scratch your nose.

The washing will be out, I'll climb the steps
to the kitchen. The pots will be unwashed.

You won't have shopped. I'll put the kettle on,
find fruit and cheese at the back of the fridge.

Neither of us will say hello.

The Gooseberry Bush

WAND

This morning, for the umpteenth time you joke
about the way my tits float in the bath
perpendicular as G.I. Jane's.
The Predictor wand's still on the floor

the purple line condensing in its window
too pale to match the reference line.
You shake off piss with a flick of the wrist
a lassoing action I'd not clocked before.

You zip. We talk about the PT Cruiser
we can't afford. Your heart's set
on Patriot Blue. I fancy Cranberry.
Something isn't happening here –

a luteinising hormone's meant to surge.
You kiss me, stroke my hair and leave.
The latch drops. I stay and soak
getting wrinkled, waiting for the steam to clear.

LATE

All night the cat's sheathed paws thump on wood,
mews trickle through my sleep as a cry
of *mum*. There's a man in my rose-print dress,
a child teeters in my mother's mules.

You snore, free-fall as if you just slipped
off me. In town a beggar compliments me
on the pendant bought in Pakistan –
the word, *heirloom*, heavy on my throat.

On the train a woman feeds her child,
its tongue malleable beneath the spoon,
blackcurrant yoghurt bilging round.
It's the smell that fully wakes me now.

The cat pauses, glares as my feet
slap to the bathroom lino. I squeeze
the pad between my legs, feel it fold
to my cunt – thick and clean and soft.

DINNER

Mary shows us photos of her daughter –
she wonders about another while she's time.
Gill and Sue agree that girls are worse –
three out of four pregnancies, sick as a dog.
John's got three beneath the age of five,
understands how people hurt them though he
never would. Paula smiles. She phoned home
just to hear hers sleep. No-one's asked.

I rehearse the casual dropping of polycystic
ovaries into talk like this. See them lumpy,
hard, landing in the Marinara sauce,
beside the buffalo wings and sea-food combo –
chairs squeak back an inch or two, napkins dab
at tomato, garlic, goo, and someone tries
to make a joke about the dangers
of eating oysters with a partner left at home.

HEAT

On Monday's scan, laid out full-bladdered
and oiled, I saw an ovum bloat its cyst
almost to bursting. Last night I slept
arse on a pillow – the smallest wet patch

in the history of our sex-life. Here
at Lord's, we've lost forty overs to the rain,
two wickets down – the ball shifts
in heavy air and somehow slips through.

The brolly's drips wick through my jeans –
I think of the ovum's slow descent
through jellyfish funnel, the sperm
blind-butting the walls around the tube.

The Ashes all but lost, we're drinking Pimms,
eating strawberries going soft
while I'd swear there's a new kind of tingle
low and left, as a slow ball is tickled to the rope.

SUN

You return from the rock two days too late,
but sometimes dawn sex needs no reason
and the Southern Comfort and ice-cubes
were a gift. Today is Sunday,

hollyhocks have grown uninvited
in the veggies. The guinea pig's on the grass
gorging itself as you would if carpet
were made of the stuff of Lemon Bonbons,

but you're in clover anyway, plucking
green tomatoes before the snails attack
and stashing them in a box with apples
to ripen. And I'm happier than expected

bundling turd-tangled straw and newspaper
soaked in musky pee. I've my hands full
arranging Shane Warne face up,
when you post a blackberry between my teeth.

LINE

It was you that told me the one about the squaw
who called her first born *Babbling Brook*, her second
Moonlit Night and then the youngest *Oh Fuck
Johnny Broke.* And you, it turns out, bought the line
about the twinkle in the father's eye,
the sex ed lie – *when two people love
each other very much* (a video
complete with moonlight and guitars). Only me
that marked up chapter seven of *McKean
Biology for Life* and only me,
that learnt the Latin names. But I was raised
on Grimm, glistened at the thought of daughters
red as blood and white as snow, dreamt up
from needlepricks and hope. You can keep
your fairy tales – as secretly I plot our child
with urine test, thermometer and chart.

SMALL HOURS

Midnight- by the window eating Aero,
humming *Lord and Father of Mankind* —
a vixen scrikes into a dark so soft
it holds her cry between the particles of air.

Undisturbed, the kink-tailed tube mice
pick at crumbs beneath the tracks, a rat
chews herself a nest from cardboard boxes.
Sometime on a night like this I'll join them

be noisy, naked underneath the moon
until someone, maybe anyone,
makes a hammock of their limbs,
and holds my bones as they were held

that airy night, when three of us
were carried car to kitchen, feigning sleep
in moth-light, and I, the heaviest
with dangling legs, my father's cargo.

BUNKER

Following signs marked Secret Nuclear Bunker,
we drive down a red earth track which winds
past fields fringed in kale and plantain
and walk through woods to a fifties farmhouse.

Orange hardboard in the wooden slots
lets us know we're on amber alert. We're led
through tank metal to offices with paintwork
of a dirty eau-de-nil I know from school.

We watch *Protect and Survive*, plan
a sandbagged refuge beneath our stairs.
Blond bobbed dummies in crimplene suits
loll near typewriters. Telexes rattle

as they did for the pools. A child has sent
a secret fax − *I love you Dad*. Tonight's
the night marked F on my calendar −
I'm sure this time I've read the signs just right.

METFORMIN

These the chalky discs that bind my cycle
to twenty-nine days, compelling my cells
to read the chemistry of my blood. Each night

the central heating rattles on and off
the washing machine whirrs through its programmes
while insulin, now acknowledged,

diminishes. The pituitary,
bobbing on currents of blood, releases streams
of FH, LSH, and ovaries bud

like coral. And so we couple frantically
on moonless nights as spring tide brings a flush
of oyster spawn to the shore. Neap tides

we chat and eat and shop until the full moon –
the earth another sector round the sun –
finds me wakeful, queasy and you and I
as distant as the south poles of magnets.

STANDING STONE

Wind-whipped, we've tromped across the moor
to the Man-y-tol – round and holed
between two uprights. I rub my thumb
over lichens – foliose and lovat green,
swallow a wish, to hear you voice a thought
I'm sure was mine. I must pass through
the eye of the stone. My fingers find a hold
on ancient granite, feet first I limbo
until my seat is firm as on the tyre
that swung the gorge between the motorway
and fields. I wiggle through, the hoops
of all those bridesmaid's petticoats
lifting above my knees, my waist, my chest.
Held between mud and cloudless sky, I see you
framed in the other world, arm ready
to take my weight on our linked hands.

OUT

The night I finally tell my mother, she says
she fell so easily they tied her tubes.
Her mother never even wanted half
of hers. We can almost smell my Nana

obese, well-buttoned, with one surprise child
at forty odd. I sleep soundly for once
in my old bed, a chink of light falling
across the carpet the way it always did.

In the morning, while I froth the milk
for coffee, she tells me that she cried for me
all night, about the time I was almost lost,
and she searched for a bean amongst the clots.

Like grief, I say, each month, and we stand
in silence, arms folded. The kettle boils.
Through the window a magpie picks its way
across the snow sprinkled on the slates.

PAINT

My father-in-law's staying in the room next door.
You won't touch me. I haven't finished
a sentence all fortnight. You've got him
decorating our would-be nursery.
I'd wanted the yellow pages ad. Bulge
in dungarees on the stepladder,
paint-splodged, craving. I might have hummed.
The job, as you say, is a good 'un.

All those fumes. An ember glows
beneath the curls of waste. A spark. A word
I meant to say. Paintwork blisters. Paper
scorches, peels away from the room
where our child was meant to lie. By the time
you wake I'm changing into fifth
screeching the corner near Bywaters
a Duplo figure plugged into my small red car.

WAIT

Sweet lemon chutney. Sharp after weeks
of wading nausea, of packing food
around my pills. I cook but never lick the spoon,
knife-scrape paths in the sandpit of my plate.

Once, I drive through a dawn that bleaches
denim. Most nights I pick my way home
down the street through scraps of greasy card
and chicken. I count us to the shortest day,

and back again. The man at the corner shop
severs a finger. We book our seats
for next years test match. I lose a silver earring
before I miss its weight. We both get flu.

Days merge like strips of coloured plasticine,
I wait for sunlight, citrus. My mother rings
to let me know it's light at six. A gosling
drags its wake through the slick of a river.

DOUBLE BED

Our bed was a secret world of Saturday nights
and Sunday mornings – scattered with crumbs
and condom foil – that faded to mine alone
throughout the week. Made solid, sacred

in those first few weeks, by marriage. We'd lie
for hours reading the words we finger-tipped
on skin. We dragged that bed two hundred miles
and now each night we share it with
your doctor, jocular as he checks
your balls. The consultant palpates my flesh,
speculum dangling by my thigh, a small nurse
strokes my shoulder as the pain grabs hold.

Next they'll draw your sperm, still wiggling
from my cervix, trap it between slide
and cover slip. Our duvet's torn aside –
we're rolled away bare-arsed, as they check our stains.

THIRTY SIX

I wear tights in summer, buy moisturiser
in pearlised pots. The phrase *no children?*
has lost its *yet*. I'm late everywhere.

The A14 slips past as I speed up
the A1. On the embankment
my feet won't stick to my mules.

In Highgate cemetery, at twilight
the gates about to close, a doll's head
life-size is skewered on a branch.

A gravestone close to Marx reads *He Takes
the Best* and I laugh: *now they tell us...*
And so the lists grow longer. Cutting bread

a child emerges in my gaze, tumbling
on grass, sure of where his gravity lies,
a small sun in his own universe.
I turn my face aside and close my eyes.

EVOLUTION

The brochures for the Galapagos have arrived.
I wonder how I'd trot those rocks five months
down the line, but soon I'm lost in Darwin's finches –
recast as parrots, warblers, woodpeckers;
tortoises that grow as big as pigs.
I'm back to my books – to the moon-faced monk
who saw that peas in pods were not alike,
and juggled their genes like beans in a bag.

The production lines of your testes roll
each night, I calculate the variations –
two to the power of forty six – fall asleep
factoring in crossover and mutation
as chromatids untangle from the mass of threads.
One Sunday lunch our friend peels back
the dressing from her hand – the new skin
pink and raw, the new lines as before.